Not since *Love Letters* has there been anything as novel, disarmingly vulnerable or captivating as *He Writes, She Writes*. Conceived spontaneously with Irwin Zahn, this new book of verse is an enchantment you will not be able to put down. – Dr. Ken Druck, Ph.D., Author, *Courageous Aging: Your Best Years Ever Reimagined*

She is a whirlwind of warmth; he is a repository of reflection. IT is a WINNER! – Patrick Riley, MD

He Writes, She Writes is one of the most beautiful books I have ever read. Once I started reading it, I couldn't put it down until I had finished it. Then I went back and re-read those poems. Some of them made me tearful while most brought a smile. Not only is each poem wonderful, but the back-and-forth [between the poets] is just lovely. – Dilip V. Jeste, MD, Distinguished Professor of Psychiatry and Neurosciences, Director, Sam and Rose Stein Institute for Research on Aging, University of California San Diego

After reading this collaboration by Natasha Josefowitz and Irwin Zahn, three descriptive words came immediately to mind: "charming," "playful" and "genteel." Without reservation, I can recommend this short book of poems by these two accomplished San Diegans. The two poets have different takes on such matters as aging, dieting, everyday sightseeing, loneliness, memories of youth, and pending death. Josefowitz and Zahn are both amiable story tellers, who mix humor and humility with insight. – Donald H. Harrison, Co-publisher, *San Diego Jewish World*

Delightful and instructive, not a bad apple in the bunch! I particularly like the interplay of the two [poets] each facing a fact of life and taking a different stance about it. – Dr. Laura Nathanson, Pediatrician and author of *The Portable Pediatrician*

Natasha's book with Irwin is brilliant! Astounded by the consistently prodigious outpourings from a fertile brain! Grateful and privileged to know her. – Robert N. Weinreb, MD, Chairman and Distinguished Professor of Ophthalmology, Director of the Shiley Eye Institute, University of California San Diego

HE WRITES,
SHE WRITES

HE WRITES, SHE WRITES

A Dialogue of Contrasting Views Written in Verse

NATASHA JOSEFOWITZ
AND
IRWIN ZAHN

© 2018 Natasha Josefowitz and Irwin Zahn
All rights reserved.

ISBN: 1975785053
ISBN 13: 9781975785055
Library of Congress Control Number: 2017913564
CreateSpace Independent Publishing Platform
North Charleston, South Carolina

DEDICATION

I dedicate this book to all the men with secret poems in their hearts. I hope this will make them brave enough to share them.
Natasha Josefowitz

This book is to encourage women to take a chance and develop their creativity, pursue it with passion, and discover themselves in the process.
Irwin Zahn

PREFACE: HOW IT ALL STARTED

THE TENNIS GAME
Natasha

He serves a male poem
she returns one
from a female perspective
he throws a ball
of raw emotions
she responds
to his adventures
with stories of her own
and so they volley
back and forth
pages facing each other
yin and yang
Mars and Venus
calling out to one another
in their eternal struggle
to understand
by sharing, comparing
explaining, describing
and finally combining
into a book

INTRODUCTIONS

Irwin

I attended a lecture, three parts light and one part serious, on aging and life after work. The talk by Natasha captured my interest and I bought a signed copy of her book, *Retirement – The Next Great Adventure*. Best of all, I read the poems, enjoyed the insights and had a warm, comforting feeling.

Natasha's lecture caught me on the edge of retiring and searching for my next direction. I contacted her, arranged a meeting, and liked her direct, no nonsense comments. We left saying we'd meet again in the future.

Some weeks later I was on a long flight returning form Europe to the West Coast. While most passengers were sleeping, or reading, or watching movies, I thought of a recent happening in Germany. I thought about it, smiling at the memory, and then with pen and paper, wrote a poem about the incident. More accurately, the poem wrote itself.

I sent the poem to Natasha who was delighted with the story, and encouraged me to write more. The rest appears on the following pages.

Natasha

The phone rings; an unfamiliar voice introduces itself.

"I am Irwin Zahn. I went to your lecture on retirement and bought your book. I am planning to sell my business and start a charitable foundation in which my three children will be involved. Would you be willing to meet with us as a consultant? Of course I'll pay whatever fee you require."

I am surprised at the request, but pleased at the opportunity to work on such an interesting project.

Within a week, I meet with Irwin and his three adult children. We discussed the various opportunities both in San Diego and elsewhere—he is mostly interested in health and education. As we leave, I give him one of my poetry books.

A few weeks later, I get a phone call asking to have breakfast with me. He comes to the White Sands La Jolla retirement community where I live and brings me a poem he wrote about his trip to Munich, Germany. He says my book inspired him to write.

I am amazed at the quality of the poem and especially at the insight and willingness to share a male fantasy—not a business man's usual talent. It triggered a poetic response in me—these are the first two poems in the book.

A week later, I get an e-mail with another poem—that one is about standing in a bus and being offered a seat. I sent a response.

And so it goes. He sends me poems by e-mail, and I e-mail him back the feminine perspective. We rarely meet; when we do it is all business—the sale of his factories, his foundation, trust funds for his grandchildren.

This book is the result of a man discovering parts of himself he did not know existed and a woman who is so taken by this disclosure that it triggered an immediate response of her own… one poet to another.

TABLE OF CONTENTS

Preface: How It All Started · ix
The Tennis Game · ix
Introductions · x

His/Her Poems · 1
A Woman on a Munich Subway · 2
A Man on the Subway · 3
Today a Woman Offered Me a Bus Seat · 4
Today I Offered My Bus Seat · 5
Movie Fantasy · 6
Making Out · 7
Who's That Old Man in the Mirror? · 8
Who Is That Old Woman in the Mirror? · 9
Gotta Get A Life · 10
"You Never Know" and "Just in Case" · 11
Chocolate Chip Cookies with the Soulful Eyes · 12
To Eat or Not To Eat · 13
I'll Name My Boat "Dream Boat" · 14
Piano Lessons · 15
I'm Wild About Steam Engines and Trains · 16
What I Like · 17
"You'll Never Amount to Anything!" · 18
What You See Is What You Get · 19

Thinking Negatively	20
Whirling Mind	21
Wings of Silver, Bars of Gold	22
When I Grow up, I Want to Be...	25
Flying Over the Ocean at Night	26
Alone at a Party	27
If I Had a Million Dollars	28
Dreams	29
Important Things	30
I Worry About the World	31
Beyond the Horizon	32
Getting There Is *All* the Fun!	33
It Started with a Dream	34
Someday...	35
Neighborhood Fire Hydrant Always Ready	36
The Drinking Fountain	37
For Every Teacher a Nobel Prize	38
The Chef	39
Ode to an Unknown French Language Teacher	40
A Teacher Who Made a Difference	43
Do I Look American?	44
Not Sounding American	45
Good, Better, Best	46
The Mantra	47
The Big Apple	48
Changing Geography	49
Lights on Broadway	50
Little Pleasures	51
Grandchildren in College	52
A Civilized Person	53
Advice to a College Graduate on a First Job	54
Advice for a First Day at Work	55
Gardening for Fun and Profit	56

Jeans: the Great Equalizers ·57
Officer, You Must Be Blind or Infirm! ·58
How to Avoid a Traffic Ticket ·61
Life's Secret ·62
New Attitude ·63
The Secret to Life · 64
My Secret ·65
Stumbling into Retirement · 66
Post-Retirement Crisis ·67
Do You Think of Your Own Mortality? · 68
Done ·69
New York Cemetery in Winter ·70
The Cemetery ·71
There Are No Tombstones in the Cemetery · · · · · · · · · · · · · · · · · · ·72
Scattered ·74
End of Life ·76
What Will I Die Of? · 77
Natasha: Active, Spirited and Alive ·78
Discovering Irwin ·79

HIS/HER POEMS

A WOMAN ON A MUNICH SUBWAY

Irwin

A woman on a Munich subway
smiled at me and at my luggage
as I struggled with the station map.
No taxi was at my subway stop
when that woman volunteered to help.

I told her my nearby destination
and she volunteered to drive me there.
With thanks, I jumped at the opportunity.
She drove and said she was shopping
and was pleased to help a stranger.

While driving I thought, should I suggest dinner?
Perhaps red wine with colorful conversation?
Could a friendship grow to a relationship?
When would circumstance return me to Munich?

Quick as a smile she brought me to my hotel.
The Munich subway woman said goodbye
and drove away taking my fantasies with her.

A MAN ON THE SUBWAY
Natasha

A man on the subway
seemed lost
studying a station map
he was looking for a taxi
when I know
there are none at this hour
I asked his destination
it was on my way
so I offered to help
he was well dressed
and quite good-looking
so I felt it would be safe
to give a stranger a lift
we chatted a bit
he seemed really nice
perhaps he would suggest
a glass of wine
or maybe even dinner
these kinds of encounters
can lead to friendships
or maybe even more
like maybe after dinner
his hotel room?
When we arrived
he thanked me and was gone
and I thought about
what could have been
but never was
what a pity

TODAY A WOMAN OFFERED ME A BUS SEAT
Irwin

Today a woman offered me a seat on the bus.
Why did she do that? And why me?
Do I appear crippled? Am I ancient?
I didn't look, but others are older than me.

What changed? I opened doors for older people.
I gave up my seat in subway cars.
I once ran a 5K race.
Took stairs to my office two at a time.

It's true, we all get older, even me.
I have a pacemaker, and my PSA is rising.
But my inside clock feels like fifty,
though I recently celebrated eighty

Maybe the bus incident was a signal.
Perhaps it is a sign that I'm becoming a senior.
No, tomorrow I'll look for some older person
to give up my seat to.

TODAY I OFFERED MY BUS SEAT
Natasha

Today I offered my bus seat
to an elderly gentleman
hanging on to the strap
standing uneasily
he seemed tired
he thanked me
but looked startled
I guess I had offended him
assuming he would be grateful
assuming that he did not see
himself as "old"
perhaps his self-image
was not the one he projected
I must be more careful next time
to only offer my seat
to more fragile looking people

MOVIE FANTASY
Irwin

I arrived at the movie theater,
seated well before the picture started.
Waiting for the movie,
I looked around the theater.
Up front was a young couple.
The woman was half facing her partner
with her hand stroking his neck.

I imagined if I were being stroked,
I wouldn't sit there waiting for the film.
Rather, I would abandon the popcorn
and quickly spirit her away with me.

We would run to a private place.
I would light her senses and then,
the theatre lights darkened, sound came on,
and the movie started.

Somewhere, that woman lives.
and I'm sure we'll never meet,
but I know in my heart,
that together we lost a great opportunity.

MAKING OUT
Natasha

I sit alone
in a movie theater
in front of me
a couple is kissing
they're not watching the movie
I feel their hunger
for each other
it reminds me
of what I'm missing
wanting an arm
around my shoulder
or a hand on my knee
a whisper in my ear
when I was young
we used to neck
in the darkness
getting excited
it's been a long time
since I thought about
making out
in a movie theater

WHO'S THAT OLD MAN IN THE MIRROR?
Irwin

It's a curious face, smaller than I thought.
The beard and what's left of the hair is white.
Ears are extended and the chin droops.
But, I find and recognize a twinkling eye.

Facial features like my older brother.
The shoulders seem narrower than I thought.
Stance is not bent, but not erect either.
It can't be me, but who is it?

I have a strong mental self image.
I've always acted younger than my age.
My eyesight is weakening, and I read less.
I'm still purposeful and vital.

Where was I when I got older?
I've always been interested and involved.
Does the mirror reflect the truth?
That old man can't be me.

I don't care what the mirror says!
Mentally I know that I'm younger,
and I'm determined to continue to act that way!

WHO IS THAT OLD WOMAN IN THE MIRROR?

Natasha

Every morning as I wake up
I brush my teeth
and look into the mirror

Every morning as I get up
I am surprised
at what is reflected in that mirror

Every morning I expect
to see this youngish face
and every morning what is there
is this rather oldish face
with more wrinkles
than I last remembered
and grayer hair than
I saw yesterday

Every morning as I brush my teeth
I shake my head in disbelief

GOTTA GET A LIFE
Irwin

Gotta exercise, gotta eat hearty.
Gotta walk, gotta return calls.
Gotta reconcile checkbook.
Gotta vote.

Gotta phone Alice, gotta visit Mike.
Gotta plan vacation, gotta go to tailor.
Gotta get groceries, gotta go to work.

Gotta go to dentist, gotta get checkup.
Gotta change the oil, gotta diet.
Gotta update cell phone and computer.

Gotta write "thank yous," gotta renew license.
Gotta Facebook, gotta Twitter.
Then, when all gottas are done
gotta leave room to enjoy living.

"YOU NEVER KNOW" AND "JUST IN CASE"

Natasha

"You never know"
and "just in case"
are the words
I live by
so I notice
what seems insignificant
and remember
unimportant events
I do some things
not for the doing
but for the having done
I collect experiences
and live through events
which are not all
especially pleasant
but I do not mind
and keep doing it
because "just in case,"
"you never know"…
something may come in handy

CHOCOLATE CHIP COOKIES WITH THE SOULFUL EYES
Irwin

There the cookie sits
Waiting with soulful eyes
Plump chocolate chips resting
In an oven-tanned dress

Sitting lonely on a plate
As if waiting for an event
An event as seen by a wide eyed child
Or a starving teenager

Accompanied by a glass of milk
Or perhaps an elegant tea service
But nothing will make this cookie
Giggle with delight until it's eaten

Dear stranger, join the cause
Take a position, do your duty
When you see this soulful cookie
Make it happy by eating it

TO EAT OR NOT TO EAT
Natasha

One cookie on a platter
its companions gone
it sits beckoning me
I had decided
to forgo sugar
stop eating saturated fats
I want to lose
a few pounds
but that cookie
with its chocolate-chip eyes
is winking at me
to eat or not to eat
that is the question
to give into temptation
or remain firm
in one's resolve
half a cookie on a platter
sits contentedly

I'LL NAME MY BOAT "DREAM BOAT"

Irwin

Some day soon I'll go sailing.
I'll take sailing lessons.
Learn everything about the wind.
Understand the mysteries of tides.

I will study navigation
and buy a marine GPS system.
Take Coast Guard classes on piloting.
Read about right-of-way with other boats.

First, I'll practice turning and docking.
Then I'll slowly explore the bay
before finally venturing into the ocean.
Of course, always within sight of the shore.

I'm going to invite family and friends.
Maybe sail to a dockside restaurant.
I'll cut the auxiliary motor and quietly sail
But first I need to raise my procrastinating anchor.

PIANO LESSONS
Natasha

Someday I'll take piano lessons
I will learn to read music
and play anything
on sheet music
someday I'll take piano lessons
and learn to play by ear
and accompany friends
who want to sing
someday I'll take piano lessons
and play for myself
all the music I have loved
from Russian gypsy songs
to French nursery rhymes
from Für Elise
to Scott Joplin
someday when I have time
I will take piano lessons

I'M WILD ABOUT STEAM ENGINES AND TRAINS
Irwin

I go way out of my way
and never pass an opportunity
to visit an old-steam-engine museum
or a railroad-car and train barn.

I'm excited with anticipation
before I even get there
and am never disappointed
no matter how skimpy or rich the display.

With trains I marvel at the size,
the breadth, enormity of the design,
the behemoth-sized freight carriers
just sitting there on display, waiting to roar.

I marvel at the mechanical ingenuity,
the vision, the talents, the skills,
that, joined together with guts and daring,
produced a working, moving miracle.

Modern-day train engines are nice,
but don't exude the driving potential
locked in these formidable steam engines.
In another life, I'll return as a trainman!

WHAT I LIKE
Natasha

I go to museums
and art galleries
I like to look at dinosaurs
and to exhibits of miniatures
I visit aquariums
and wild-animal parks
botanical gardens
old churches and graveyards
I marvel at toy trains
that run on intricate tracks
and Christmas store-window displays
I look into arts and crafts shops
I enjoy planetariums
I wander through science fairs
I browse through the volumes
of second-hand bookstores
the only places
I will never go
to are old steam-engine museums
and railroad-car and train barns

"YOU'LL NEVER AMOUNT TO ANYTHING!"
Irwin

My father said, "you'll never amount to anything."
When I cut classes and didn't do homework,
teacher said I was a disturbing influence
and demanded a meeting with my mother.

Mother was the loving, nurturing parent.
Father the strong, structured, rigid disciplinarian.
There were penalties, loss of perks,
Restrictions, etc., all to little avail.

Somehow, I struggled through the school system,
doing minimum work, barely hanging on.
Fifty plus years have passed.
Mother and father are long gone.

After a few industry jobs, I moved
into my own start-up business.
I kept moving to larger and larger quarters
and slowly expanded to overseas locations.

Today the business is strong and thriving.
I'm certain it grew at expense of family.
In retrospect, did I show my father
that I really amounted to something?

WHAT YOU SEE IS WHAT YOU GET
Natasha

While my father wore an ascot to breakfast
and my mother came to dinner in a long dress
I arrived in a sweat suit and bare feet
my mother used silver and china to set the table
I plunked down a milk carton
my mother fussed over leftovers
to make them look attractive
I ate out of the plastic containers they were stored in
my mother wrote fancy thank-you notes
I left a message on the phone
hoping the people would be out
while my parents looked elegant out on a walk
I wore sneakers and something old and comfy
my mother put on makeup carefully every morning
I usually forgot to even put lipstick on
I was the bane of my parents' existence
and my appearance always made them sigh loudly
since I could never measure up, I had given up trying
what you see is what you get
and that was never good enough
and now that I am in my nineties
I sometimes wonder what my mother would say
I still catch myself trying to please her

THINKING NEGATIVELY
Irwin

Sometimes, when lying in bed,
the mind reviews negative events:
a hurtful remark,
a loved one's medical problems.

Not only when trying to sleep,
but alone in quiet reflection,
a sad event intrudes into our thoughts
and our thinking spirals downwards.

Within us, we have the solution.
We're in charge, just change the image.
Imagine billowing clouds
or a Hawaiian beach scene.

Picture a baby playing in a bathtub,
an elderly couple holding hands.
Our minds are the tools
that can give us control.

WHIRLING MIND
Natasha

Oh mind of mine,
switch to happier thoughts
turn away, oh brain,
from negative images
stop, racing heart,
leave the scary memories
do not shake,
trembling hand,
restore calm
remember a better place
conjure an image
that will heal
so stop, oh mind,
from whirling so

.

WINGS OF SILVER, BARS OF GOLD

Irwin

Years ago, when I was in high school
World War II was raging on.
A patriotic war, with a great cause,
and I couldn't wait to get in.

The dominant topic in the senior class was enlisting.
Bold, macho types wanted to join the Marines.
Conservative souls chose the Coast Guard.
The air was abuzz with service choices.

Propaganda efforts were everywhere.
"Loose lips, sink ships"
printed onto posters illustrating a sinking ship.
One colorful, effective poster grabbed my attention.

It showed a dashing pilot, complete with white scarf
with fighter planes swooping in the background
and pretty women admiring the officer.
Underneath, "Wings of Silver, Bars of Gold."

My imagination flew higher than the planes,
Transporting me into a trim officer's uniform
with silver pilot's wings, and lieutenant's gold bars,
and, of course, the bevy of admiring girls.

I enlisted as a cadet in the Army Air Corps.
Soon, I received a form letter.
The flying program was canceled.
The war was going well; they had enough pilots.

I always visit airplane museums in my travels
and look skyward when I hear low-flying planes.
But deep within my core, bursting to get out
is the uniformed pilot with white scarf and admiring girls.

WHEN I GROW UP, I WANT TO BE...
Natasha

I wrote poetry as a child
as many children do
and dreamed of being a poet
and traveling the world over
reading my poems
to enthralled audiences
then I grew up
and became an author
of business books
each chapter
started with a poem
which I then could read
to large audiences
as I traveled the world over
leading business seminars
fulfilling my early dreams

FLYING OVER THE OCEAN AT NIGHT

Irwin

It's quiet, the passengers are asleep.
I feel the aircraft's forward motion.
Which direction is it going?
For what end or purpose?

Plowing through the skies,
It seems to be flying by itself.
Where is it going? When will it get there?
For what end or purpose?

Will it keep flying forever
until the fuel is exhausted?
Is there a specific location
we are headed to?

Will the plane land on a magic island
with people welcoming us
with smiles and flowers?
Or with frowns and guns?

Soon there's a shaking, rumbling
followed by the captain's announcement,
something to do with seatbelts.
Will there be friendly people or warriors
on landing?

I do not know.

ALONE AT A PARTY
Natasha

Going alone to a party
will the people there be friendly?
will someone talk to me
or will I stand in a corner
glass in hand?
scanning the room
for a familiar face
not finding one
looking for a smile or nod
approaching close-knit groups
unable to enter
I am a stranger among the natives
an alien in a foreign land
I will go home early tonight

IF I HAD A MILLION DOLLARS
Irwin

When I was a child
I had lots of dreams.
In the dreams I had a million dollars
then I could do anything I wished.

I could go to exotic places,
hire private planes and yachts
and then travel everywhere
like the French Riviera or Hong Kong.

When I grew older
I thought if I had a million
I would buy a ski lodge
or a cottage on a lake.

Years have passed.
I now have the million dollars,
but prefer to stay home
close to friends and family.

Early dreams of having money,
then with money different dreams
The true dreams
are in our own backyard.

DREAMS
Natasha

Two childhood dreams:
becoming a well-known poet
and being madly in love
I became that poet
and married that love
and now that he is dead
what is left
are the poems

It will have to do

IMPORTANT THINGS
Irwin

I'd like to do something big.
Something really noteworthy.
I'd like to summon a peace conference.
I want to settle the Iraq situation.

Feed the starving African children.
Find a cure for cancer.
Stop and reverse global warming.
Solve the Israeli/Arab mess.

I'm destined for important things.
I can make tough, difficult decisions.
I'm an extinguisher looking for a fire.
Give me a problem, and I'll solve it.

But instead I'm consumed with drivel.
Fix the washer, clean the garage.
Service the car, buy light bulbs.
I'm wasted, I'm made for better.

But, for all the grandiose visions
I've led a full life.
I was honest and caring
and stood true to my values.

I guess it will have to do.

I WORRY ABOUT THE WORLD
Natasha

I worry about the ozone layer and acid rain
I worry about the destruction
of the Amazon rain forest
about the possibility of a nuclear disaster
and the depletion of our fossil fuels

I worry about the endangered species
and the pollution of our oceans
about overpopulation and gang violence
about famine in Africa
war in the Middle East
the federal deficit
the peace negotiations
I worry and feel so helpless
about our earth, our country, our streets

So in the meantime
I'll call my mother more often
be there for my family
look in on my neighbor
take care of a friend
support worthwhile causes
be honest and outspoken

In the meantime
what I can do is
start improving the world
in my own backyard

BEYOND THE HORIZON
Irwin

What will I discover
beyond the horizon?
Are there other mountains to climb?
Are there deserts to cross?

What am I searching for?
New buildings to build?
More companies to grow?
Leaving a legacy?

I'm always speeding,
running on an obsessive quest.
Is there something
that is always beyond my reach?

I know the answer.
It's always there, but never seen.
That elusive, hidden "something"
Is the journey!

GETTING THERE IS *ALL* THE FUN!
Natasha

I have always tried to do it all
to become a better person
to acquire the sufficient knowledge
the necessary skills
the right attitude

And when I have accomplished it
finally made it
or know just about enough
to feel I have arrived

I set my eyes again
on some new, distant goal
working hard
to get to that next
arrival place

So I have come to realize
that it is not the destination
that matters
but the journey

IT STARTED WITH A DREAM
Irwin

Dayton Ohio was a bicycle town
with many shops and factories.
Orville and Wilbur had a bike shop
complete with a tool room in the back.

Together, they began experimenting
with building and flying kites.
They built, modified and tested
and learned flying features.

The dream was for man to fly
so they built and rebuilt large kite frames
that would hold a person and
and finally at Kitty Hawk they flew.

But staying aloft needed power
which meant designing new propellers
and developing light weight engines,
all connected with bicycle chains.

Overcoming crashes and injuries,
changing traditional design principals,
innovating new control devices,
they triumphed with powered flight.

These two brothers from Dayton Ohio
changed the lives of everyone everywhere
with their remarkable invention
and it all started with a dream!

SOMEDAY…
Natasha

People with dreams
unfulfilled
someday I will…
someday I hope to…
someday maybe…
when I have time
when I have
finished working
finished raising the children
finished fixing up the house
then
that day
may be too late

NEIGHBORHOOD FIRE HYDRANT ALWAYS READY

Irwin

Standing fully alert, always ready!
You felt children jump over you.
Assorted dogs and cats defining their territories.
Through sun, snow and fog, always ready!

You watch those playful children
grow, learn to drive, marry and leave.
Over long years, the neighborhood changed
in different ways, but you're always ready!

Drivers park illegally next to you.
Street cleaning equipment washed over you.
Teenagers decorated you with spray paints.
Through it all, you were there, always ready!

A long time ago you helped put out a fire.
It saved a family and property as well.
Never rewarded nor praised,
but happy, satisfied, and always ready!

THE DRINKING FOUNTAIN
Natasha

In parks and hospitals
in museums and office buildings
in theater lobbies
drinking fountains
usually too low
always uncomfortable
bending down to get a mouthful
careful not to touch the spout
in France, where I grew up,
there was a metal cup
attached by a chain
to the bowl
the homeless man drank from it
and also the children
my mother used to rinse the cup
before filling it for me
no one worried about germs
perhaps they had not been invented
the water fountains of the world
quenching the world's thirst

FOR EVERY TEACHER A NOBEL PRIZE
Irwin

Mother was raised in European traditions.
The male breadwinner was treated as king.
The separation of duties was rigid and unequal.
He brought home a salary; she did everything else.

She brought up the children, helped with the homework,
cooked the meals, prepared the school sandwiches.
She did the sewing and bought clothes for the children.
Always visited the teachers and went to school meetings.

Mother loved writing and was an excellent student.
Always volunteered for recording secretary assignments
with charitable, school and religious groups
and, sometimes found time for reading.

She loved reading aloud to her children.
Attended lectures, and read reports.
Mother thought the highest calling,
that nothing would surpass, is teaching.

Imagine the satisfaction, the pure joy
of sharing knowledge, improving abilities,
raising capabilities and growing minds.
Every teacher should get a Nobel Prize.

THE CHEF
Natasha

She shops at the market
filling her cart
dragging small children
drives back home
carries the heavy bags
fills the fridge
cooks the vegetables
marinates the steak
chops the salad
mashes the potatoes
bakes the pie
sets the table
calls everyone to sit down
he dons the apron
places the steaks on the grill
turns them over once
he is the chef
she is his helper

ODE TO AN UNKNOWN FRENCH LANGUAGE TEACHER
Irwin

I was a bored, turned-off teenager
taking a high school French language course.
The droning of the teacher
only quickened my dreams of escape.

Circling the classroom walls
were standard French tourist posters.
The Eiffel Tower, the mandatory Arc De Triomphe
and the awesome Mont St. Michel.

In the flatlands of northern France
stands an outcropping of rock that
becomes an island when the tides come in.
Atop, an imposing monastery.

The long forgotten French language teacher
spoke of an unusual restaurant
named Mère Poulard at the island's base
and the house specialty was an omelet.

The omelet, with its secret ingredients,
was revealed only to a very favored few.
My fantasy pictured a dying grandmother
whispering the recipe to a grandchild.

Not too many years later
I was in the Army, stationed in France.
The war had stopped and with borrowed jeep
I made my way to Mont St Michel.

With great delight the towering monastery,
higher than I imagined, was waiting for me.
The streets were bare and the stores were shuttered,
but, the Mère Poulard restaurant was open.

Of course, I ordered that omelet
and what possibly could be special?
As I watched, the egg mixture in a copper pan
was placed in a wood-burning fireplace.

The ritual-like beating of the eggs
sounded like a drum cadence,
the mixture frothed and bubbled until done.
The omelet was a glorious taste experience.

Some years later, I revisited Mère Poulard with my wife.
In subsequent times I brought my children and friends.
While my French language skills never improved,
I'll always be thankful to that unknown French teacher!

A TEACHER WHO MADE A DIFFERENCE
Natasha

My high school called
and said I was inducted
into their Hall of Fame
and could I tell them
who was my favorite teacher
it was Miss Touton, I said
I took her radio class
when I was a freshman in 1940
an eager French girl with red hair
white knee socks
and inappropriate smocked, silk dresses
my mother made me wear to school
my English was not yet good enough
but she gave me parts to play
used my scripts, had me direct them
and we actually went on the air
every Saturday morning
on an L.A. station
I owe it to her that I lost my fear
of public speaking
of being on the air
and later on television
I called her to tell her
how important
she had been in my life—
she said she remembered me!

DO I LOOK AMERICAN?
Irwin

Recently I was in France and Germany.
I noticed, with surprise,
that hotel and restaurant people
spoke to me in English.
How did they guess that I'm an American?

While I was born in Brooklyn,
how, before I spoke, did they know?
What was the giveaway clue?
Was it the cut or color of my clothes?

I know some high school French,
and am familiar with French menus.
I can say "bonjour" and "merci"
with a good accent.

But, I never had the chance.
I felt thwarted and disappointed.
Like a spy whose disguise is discovered.
But, I'll get back at them.
Next time I'll vacation in California.

NOT SOUNDING AMERICAN
Natasha

I was born in Paris
but we spoke Russian at home
and I had a German governess
they called me the Russian girl
we sailed to the States
escaping the War
I spoke no English
I was called the French girl
I married and lived in Switzerland
where I was known as the American woman
returning to the States
teaching at the University of New Hampshire
they called me the Swiss lady
I speak the Russian my mother taught me
the tsarist, classical Russian
no longer in use
my French has a Swiss lilt
and my English
has a French accent
so wherever I go
I am from somewhere else
whatever I speak, it's with an accent
whenever I talk
people ask me where I'm from
and now that I'm in California
I just say how far back
do you want to know?

GOOD, BETTER, BEST
Irwin

Good, better, best
never let it rest
'til your good is better
and your better's best!

It is a verse my mother
taught me and repeated.
It is a simple rhyme
with a catchy message.

Over the many, long years
and on the right occasion,
I repeated this quatrain to my children
and they use it as well.

Some of life's delights come unexpectedly
as when my young granddaughter
surprised me with, good better best.
My mother would have smiled!

THE MANTRA
Natasha

Every day, in every way
I'm getting better and better

My mother made me repeat this
every night before I went to bed
it was a Dr. Coué in France
whose belief was
that it would make a difference
and so I told my children
that every day
they're getting better
and my grandchildren
without this mantra
are getting better
just on their own

THE BIG APPLE
Irwin

Hordes of people, young and old
walking, rushing, pushing, shoving.
Going every which way and no way.
It's the Big Apple.

The noises, sounds, sirens, tumult.
Signs blinking, screaming, pulsating.
Sales, lowest, reduced, half prices.
It's the Big Apple.

Office buildings compete as to which is higher.
Street vendors yelling for attention.
Trash overflowing sidewalks, potholed streets.
It's the Big Apple.

Theaters everywhere.
Classical, jazz, folk concerts daily.
Delightful museums for every interest.
It's the Big Apple.

Restaurants for every appetite and pocketbook.
Various transport: subways, buses, taxis.
Parks with lovers, children, old people, and pigeons.
It's the Big Apple.

CHANGING GEOGRAPHY
Natasha

When I was young
I used to love New York
constant excitement
was in the air
I saw all the plays
went to concerts
visited museums
was part of the art crowd
my children grew up
in Central Park
New York was my city
I belonged
and now, half a century later
I live in a village
where nothing much happens
it's quiet at night
at the local market
the cashier knows my name
there is a main street
a small museum, a few restaurants
one hardware store and a movie theater
I greet all the people at the coffee shop
no one is anonymous here
I used to love New York
but now I love La Jolla

LIGHTS ON BROADWAY
Irwin

The ultimate show business recognition
was to have your name in "lights on Broadway."
Few of our names will be lit up,
but, all of us need recognition.

It doesn't require medals, the Nobel Prize
a story on TV nor your photo in the newspaper
We need a hug or an arm around the shoulder
a warm smile, a positive phrase.

We all have the magic ability
to light up a moment for someone
with a word or a glance
that signals we care, we recognize.

LITTLE PLEASURES
Natasha

I will never win the Nobel Prize, nor the Pulitzer
I will never get an Oscar, nor an Emmy
I will never be on the cover of Time magazine
or cited for anything world shaking

So I will have to make do
with getting excited
about finding a parking space
getting served quickly in a restaurant
not standing in line at the movies

I will find pleasure in a walk with my dog
the sound of birds in the morning
a bowl of hot soup by the fireplace
a glass of iced tea on a summer day

I will appreciate
a kiss, a smile, a good joke
a phone call from a friend
my kids remembering my birthday

Come to think of it
I don't need a Pulitzer or an Oscar
for I have an award far greater than these…
the sweet names of family and friends
to call on at any time

GRANDCHILDREN IN COLLEGE
Irwin

Why do they take French poetry
or nutrition in Medieval times?
How does the study of aborigines
strengthen the mind?

Yes, it's nice to review
ancient medical practices and
comparative religions,
but to what end?

But college is more than getting by,
more than some interesting courses.
Rather, it needs to spark and awaken
a drive and a passion for progress.

How do we seed in young people
The desire to find the cure
for cancer or diabetes
or to eliminate poverty?

I say au revoir to French poetry!

A CIVILIZED PERSON
Natasha

French poetry
Italian opera
Greek philosophy
English history
contemporary art
what makes a person educated?
what classes or books
should be part of one's knowledge?
what is a civilized person?
Santayana said,
"Those who cannot remember the past
are condemned to repeat it."
art, literature, music
history, geography
are the essential ingredients
of an educated person

ADVICE TO A COLLEGE GRADUATE ON A FIRST JOB
Irwin

You're starting on a new adventure
filled with surprises, fears and rewards.
You overcame the rigors of college
and are beginning a new life phase.

The people, the places, everything is new.
You dress to a new standard,
conform to new rules and regulations,
and join into an established organization.

Into your life comes a boss.
You're assigned to his group
and you join his team, now
your responsibility is to perform.

The one sure and certain way
to perform in an organization
and catch the attention of management
is to follow this simple advice.

"Do a little bit more!"
Go beyond completing the assigned task.
Fill in the necessary "next" steps.
Strike out and do more than what is asked!

ADVICE FOR A FIRST DAY AT WORK
Natasha

Share little
observe a lot
ask questions
note answers
figure out
who makes decisions
do not accept friendship
too quickly
they may be
the wrong kind of friends
read the manuals
talk to secretaries
be silent at meetings
until you know for sure
that what you say
is relevant
try to fit in at first
then later, stand out
become visible
find out what's lacking
then offer to help
be careful at first
then be innovative
but most important
be needed

GARDENING FOR FUN AND PROFIT
Irwin

There's an invisible line between
work and pleasure, duty and enjoyment.
Some folks can't wait for the weekends
to dig in the dirt and garden.

Other folks hate it when Monday arrives
and they need to garden for a living.
There are chefs that toil daily
and amateurs who love cooking

What a wonderful world this would be
if we could put everyone in a bowl,
spin it 'til properly mixed
and come out with happily satisfied people.

JEANS: THE GREAT EQUALIZERS
Natasha

Blue-collar workers wear jeans on the job
and dress up for the weekend
executive wear suits to work
and wear jeans on the weekend
blue jeans are our greatest social equalizers

OFFICER, YOU MUST BE BLIND OR INFIRM!
Irwin

A police officer with a negative attitude
stopped me and asked if I
knew the speed limit on the bridge?
And, did I realize how fast I was going?

I respectfully replied, about 45 mph.
The authority responded with "76 mph."
I said I traveled the bridge daily,
lived nearby and requested a warning.

He answered with a brief, "license and registration"
and added a mortician-like "please."
The officer returned with a ticket,
then said something about a number to call.

Officer, you must be blind or infirm!
You're a danger to other drivers.
Start wearing stronger eyeglasses,
stop driving a police car if you cant' see.

My anger rose as I replayed the event
and listed what combative actions I should take.
Some thoughts even had criminal intent, but
soon the revenge changed and disappeared.

I stopped wasting empty angry moments
and returned again to the good feeling,
happy with my ability
and continued on my way, wiser.

HOW TO AVOID A TRAFFIC TICKET
Natasha

I was driving along
not focusing on
the numbers
on my dashboard
a siren—I stopped
the police officer claimed
I was going too fast
I looked bereft
apologized
said it was terrible
that I went over
the speed limit
I thanked him
so glad he stopped me
I wasn't paying attention
from now, I will, of course
I smiled anxiously
looking guilty
he gave me a warning
and I sped away
relieved, but also
more careful

LIFE'S SECRET
Irwin

What are the secrets to this life?
Are there magic pills
that make you strong and healthy
and make every day warm and sunny?

Something to take away the gloom
of a boring job or task
or a drink you can take when you can't sleep
or you worry through the night?

Can't solve growing money problems?
Not tall enough; belly too big?
Too masculine? Too short?
Nose too big? Thinning hair?

Rush, don't walk; here's the key!
It is hidden inside all of us
and it's been there all the time.
The three things are attitude, attitude, attitude.

NEW ATTITUDE
Natasha

Today I have decided
that I am not half a couple
mourning the part that's gone
I am a whole person
standing on my own two feet
independent and strong
there is nothing I cannot do
for there is nothing I can't imagine
I have no fears, not of living, nor of dying
I feel the wisdom of my years
as my life draws to an end
I savor the moments in ways new to me
a quietness has taken hold
like a new distance, a perspective
an understanding
I know not exactly of what
a comfort in my place, a knowing of my time
the word may be "serene"
it exists in new adventures
in willingness for risks
in shoulder shrugs at failures
in smiles at foibles and secret laughter
at the amazingness of it all

THE SECRET TO LIFE
Irwin

I know some friends and family
whom I meet from time to time.
I never ask how they feel
for I'll only receive a load of complaints.

The wealthy business people I meet,
usually at golf clubs or resorts,
are forever lamenting the problems
of high taxes and politics.

Educators and teachers have
budget and discipline problems.
Airlines have ongoing
fuel and personnel problems.

Seems like every endeavor, everywhere
is filled with people carrying burdens
much of which is beyond their control.
But, the secret to this life, and
something you can control, is ATTITUDE.

Cloudy days are followed by sunshine.
It's the springtime in your mind,
not the one on the calendar, that counts.
A positive attitude is life's great secret!

MY SECRET
Natasha

Keep focused
think positive
face uncertainty as a challenge
face pain
as temporary
grieve and heal
moving forward
when the going gets tough
shouting to myself, "Showtime"
presenting a good face
to the world
"faire bonne figure"
they say in France
pretending
becomes reality
the brain believes
the lie
and turns it
into a truth
for a while anyway
try it
it works

STUMBLING INTO RETIREMENT
Irwin

I don't remember when it began,
but I started to work less
and to vacation more.
I also stopped working late.

Instead, I thought more about
going to daytime lectures and museum visits.
I began to make time for house chores
and to meet friends and children for lunch.

At some point I stopped taking work home.
I also dress more casually
and make office rounds less frequently.
Other people were making my usual decisions.

I was in the center of my work universe.
Now someone else is doing it all.
Everyone's time to move on is different.
Crying and screaming or gliding gracefully
we all must "move on" sooner or later.
I'm not retiring—I'm changing direction!

POST-RETIREMENT CRISIS
Natasha

No alarm clocks
no gulped-down coffee
not stuck in traffic
afraid to be late
no preparations
for a lecture
no office hours
nor student papers
to grade

I have retired
from full-time teaching
I am retired
from my identity
What will replace
my useful days?
How will I fill
the empty hours?

So I joined five boards
became a member
of two service clubs
learned to do healing touch
and volunteered at the ICU
at my local hospital

Joined a book club
took piano lessons
and became more frantic
than I was before

I need a vacation

DO YOU THINK OF YOUR OWN MORTALITY?

Irwin

A relative of mine died recently.
I attended the burial service
with family at the gravesite.
It was a somber, sobering experience.
As I watched the proceedings,
physically there, but mentally apart,
I began to think of my own mortality.
One day, it will be my turn.
Am I ready? Have I left things undone?
Are those close to me taken care of?
Will they be saddened and tearful?
Are there gaps? Instructions to be left?
Who will remember me? Who will care?
What legacy am I leaving?
It has been an eventful journey,
sprinkled with the normal ups and downs.
Life is really a book of experiences
family, work, joy and growth.
Altogether it's been a great story
with the last chapter still unwritten.
So seize the day, take a chance.
Grab the initiative, make it count.
Improve the lot of family and community
and make the last pages your best!

DONE
Natasha

I am getting old
it is the last moment
to make a difference
my last chance
to do that last bit of
unfinished business
but what is it
that is still left undone?
what hasn't been said?
where should I still go?
who should I see?
I don't have any regrets
I don't even have remorse
I would relive my life
the same way—with only minor changes
so if I don't know
the answers to these questions
then I must indeed be done
with no projects in sight
no mountains to climb
no passions to pursue
I am done

NEW YORK CEMETERY IN WINTER
Irwin

A dark, cold community
where everything is grey and somber.
Sky is grey, tombstones grey, trees grey.
This is a foreboding village.

Tombstones carry names and dates
of the elderly, as well as the young
all clustered in family groups.
The bushes are shivering in the wind.

All is lonely, flowers are gone.
Some tombstones have pebbles or rocks
left by friends or relatives.
The cold is biting, and nothing moves.

I see markers with dates of birth and death.
Some of the ages are close to my own.
When my time comes, I'll have on my marker,
"I'd rather be in San Diego!"

THE CEMETERY
Natasha

There is a grave marker
with my mother's name
next to one
with my father's too
a mound of earth
where my husband lies
there is a space
with grass undisturbed
waiting to be
dug up for me
there is a tree
birds are singing
I'm glad to know
where I will be

THERE ARE NO TOMBSTONES IN THE CEMETERY

Irwin

When I was a boy growing up
I was interested in studies and sports.
When I entered the workforce
I was consumed with growth and pay.

I married and started a family
and took care of a wife and children.
But all those years, never delving deeper
into my father's background and beginnings.

He was born in a tiny village
in what was then Austria-Hungary Empire.
At sixteen he came to New York City,
found a job, learned the language and
married my mother.

Many years after he died.
I got to thinking about his beginnings
and decided to visit this village
where, in some ways, I'm connected.

The town of Kozlov, population 2500,
is in the Ukraine near the Polish border.
The village sign is in Cyrillic characters
where my guide drove and interpreted.

The one street village, with chickens crossing
has ugly, rundown Russian housing.
There are few cars, and stores are located in houses.
Streets are grey, houses and people also grey.

With an interpreter I went to the town hall.
The mayor was too young to be knowledgeable,
but there was an old, angry woman
who agreed to show us the town.

She preferred to walk and not ride.
She was angry because
she had a pension with the Russians,
but nothing with the Ukrainians.

She pointed to empty, overgrown lots
where Jewish people lived.
She spoke of the devastations by the
German, Russian and Ukrainian armies.

I asked to be shown the cemetery.
There might be a familiar grave marker.
This rough, overgrown area had
rocks and markers, but no tombstones.

After the war, the destitute survivors
Used the stones as foundations for their homes.

Somewhere in that forlorn village
generations of my family are buried.
It is a miracle that my sixteen year old father
took a chance and made it possible
for me to start a better life.

SCATTERED
Natasha

My grandfather's grave
is in Berlin
having fled Russia and the communists

his oldest son
my mother's brother
not able to escape
with the rest of the family
is buried in Moscow

my other grandfather and grandmother
shot by German soldiers
are in an unmarked grave
somewhere in Lithuania

my mother's mother is buried in New York
my mother's sister rests in a grave in Paris
my parents are buried in Los Angeles
my husband lies underground in San Diego
there is a place there
for me next to him

my brother
six years younger than I
is in a grave in Scarsdale
my son is buried in Switzerland
he was sixty years old

and so we're all scattered
remnants of families
remnants of wars of immigrations
gone are the people
and soon will be gone
the memories, too

there will be
no one to remember them
not even where they are buried
and then there will be no one
to remember me

END OF LIFE
Irwin

Most times I avoid thinking
about the end of life.
I have always thought, I want
to leave in peace, with grace and dignity.

But, in truth, I really want more.
I want to go mentally alert
Not suffering pain, not kept alive,
and not burdening family and friends.

When doctors say there is no recovery
I don't want resuscitation or ventilators,
or chemo or experimental treatments.
I want to live, not be kept alive.

To those I love and are near
it is vital to say, "I love you."
To friends and relations
I want to say my goodbyes.

To those that I have angered or hurt
I am going to settle, forgive and forget.
When I can do all those things
I'll leave at peace, with grace and dignity.

WHAT WILL I DIE OF?
Natasha

What will I die of?
a silent heart attack
in the middle of the night
certainly not a stroke
that would leave me paralyzed
no, I will die of old age
knowing ahead
when the time is near
so that I will be able to
throw out all these old files
look through the photo albums
pick out the best for the grandchildren
give away my books, distribute my clothes
tell everyone goodbye

I have loved well, been loved
raised two children
who have raised my four grandchildren
and now three great-grandsons
helped some friends, hurt some others
done the best I knew how

so I have no regrets
not even remorse
I will go in peace
having celebrated the journey
but in the meantime
I better start throwing out
all these old files

NATASHA: ACTIVE, SPIRITED AND ALIVE

Irwin

Natasha with twinkling eyes,
forever active, spirited and alive,
a Niagara of projects, pursuits,
a whirlwind of activities.

Never resting or dawdling,
but with skill and direction
organizing, speaking,
writing with passion.

Her appetites, wide as her interests:
people, music, art, desserts.
She turns reflections into poetry,
poetry that kindles and provokes.

What a remarkable gift!
To observe the unusual and the mundane
and to synthesize and draw meaning
into words from unspoken thoughts.

With a quick smile, bouncing demeanor,
a devilish sense of humor,
she speeds, non-stop, through the day
active, spirited, and alive.

DISCOVERING IRWIN
Natasha

A business man correctly dressed
takes my arm to cross the street,
opens car doors
pulls out my chair in a restaurant

Irwin
straight-laced, no-nonsense
logical, rational, bright and savvy

Irwin
with a mischievous look, a secret smile,
embracing life
generous, caring and curious

Irwin
the businessman writes poetry
poetry with feelings, exposing secret fantasies
and vulnerabilities

Irwin
willing to reveal himself
and go to new places within
opening unknown doors to new adventures

Irwin
the business man transformed into
Irwin, the poet

Made in the USA
Columbia, SC
19 January 2018